SLEEP MANTRA

HOW TO SLEEP IN 9 SECONDS?

AISWARYA SOMAN

Made with ♥ on the Notion Press Platform
www.notionpress.com

To Nathaniel Kleitman, the father of sleep whose pioneering spirit illuminated the mysteries of the night, guiding us through the depths of REM and the rhythms of rest. Your dedication to unraveling the secrets of slumber has forever shaped our understanding of rest and rejuvenation.

Contents

Preface

Welcome to the enigmatic world of sleep—a journey each of us embarks on nightly, yet often takes for granted. In this book, we uncover the secrets of slumber, exploring how to quickly achieve restorative rest. From ancient calming rituals to modern scientific breakthroughs, prepare to uncover a wealth of insights, tips, and techniques to master the art of falling asleep effortlessly. Whether you seek serenity amid a bustling world or wish to unlock your mind's creative potential, join us as we explore the profound mysteries of the night. It's time to embrace the beauty of sleep and wake up to a refreshed world.

Prologue

Nathaniel Kleitman was a pioneering physiologist known for his groundbreaking research on sleep. Born in 1895 in Ukraine and later immigrating to the United States, Kleitman dedicated his career to understanding the intricacies of our nightly rest.

In the 1920s, Kleitman began his research at the University of Chicago, where he conducted some of the earliest experiments on sleep patterns. His most significant discovery came in 1953 when he identified and named REM (rapid eye movement) sleep—a phase characterized by vivid dreams and increased brain activity. This finding revolutionized our understanding of sleep cycles, distinguishing REM sleep from non-REM sleep and highlighting its importance for mental processing and learning.

Kleitman also studied the effects of environmental factors on sleep, such as light and temperature, and explored the biological rhythms that govern our sleep-wake cycles. His research laid the foundation for modern sleep medicine and neuroscience, influencing fields ranging from psychology to medicine.

Beyond his scientific achievements, Kleitman's passion for unraveling the mysteries of sleep inspired generations of researchers to delve deeper into the science of rest and its profound impact on human health and well-being. His legacy continues to shape how we understand and approach sleep today.

CHAPTER I

Introduction

Definition of Sleep

Sleep, a fundamental aspect of human existence, has captivated the curiosity of scholars, philosophers, and scientists across the ages. Defined as a natural and recurring state of altered consciousness, sleep remains a complex phenomenon with a rich history of interpretation. This in-depth exploration delves into the diverse definitions of sleep, drawing from historical perspectives, contemporary scientific insights, and the profound impact it has on our well-being.

A Historical Odyssey

Ancient Wisdom and Mysticism

The concept of sleep has deep roots in ancient wisdom and mysticism, often intertwined with spiritual and metaphysical beliefs. In ancient cultures such as the Egyptian, Greek, and Hindu civilizations, sleep was seen as a bridge between the earthly and divine realms. Quotes from ancient texts reveal a poetic understanding of sleep:

> *"Sleep is the golden chain that ties health and our bodies together."*
> *- Thomas Dekker*

In Greek mythology, Hypnos, the god of sleep, was revered for his ability to bring rest to gods and mortals alike, highlighting sleep's universal importance. Across cultures, rituals and practices evolved to honor sleep, reflecting its role in maintaining physical health and spiritual well-being. From the Renaissance to the Enlightenment, scientific inquiry into sleep began unraveling its mysteries, paving the way for modern understanding and medical advancements.

Medieval Notions: Sleep as a Passive State

During the medieval period, sleep was often regarded as a passive state, a necessary interruption in the wakeful pursuit of daily life. Quotes from medieval philosophers and scholars reflect this perception:

> *"Sleep is a temporary death; death is a perpetual sleep." - Thomas Browne*

Medieval thinkers, influenced by both classical and religious traditions, conceptualized sleep as a temporary cessation of worldly engagements, a respite from the challenges of the mortal realm.

Renaissance Awakening: Emerging Scientific Inquiry

The Renaissance marked a pivotal era where scientific inquiry began to challenge and complement existing philosophical and theological views. Scholars like Leonardo da Vinci and René Descartes initiated a shift toward understanding sleep through anatomical and physiological lenses. This era saw the emergence of early scientific explanations for sleep:

The idea of sleep as a physiological process gained traction, laying the groundwork for future advancements in sleep science.

Sleep in the Modern Era

Electroencephalography (EEG) and Sleep Stages

With the advent of modern neuroscience and technology, the mid-20th century witnessed breakthroughs in understanding sleep through the introduction of electroencephalography (EEG). The discovery of distinct sleep stages, including REM (Rapid Eye Movement) and non-REM, revolutionized the definition of sleep. Contemporary scientific insights into the brain's activity during sleep have reshaped our understanding:

> *"Sleep is the most innocent creature there is and a sleepless man the most guilty." - Franz Kafka*

Sleep, once seen as a passive state, is now recognized as a dynamic and orchestrated process, each stage contributing uniquely to physical and mental restoration.

Sleep Medicine and Disorders

The field of sleep medicine emerged, addressing sleep disorders that afflict millions worldwide. Sleep apnea, insomnia, and parasomnias are now recognized as conditions with profound implications for health. Case studies of individuals grappling with sleep disorders offer poignant narratives:

> *"A good laugh and a long sleep are the best cures in the doctor's book." - Irish Proverb*

These case studies highlight the real-world impact of sleep-related issues on individuals' lives, emphasizing the crucial role sleep plays in overall well-being.

Interdisciplinary Perspectives: Psychosocial and Cognitive Aspects

In the 21ˢᵗ century, interdisciplinary research explores the psychosocial and cognitive dimensions of sleep. From the effects of sleep on mood regulation to its role in memory consolidation, contemporary definitions of sleep extend beyond the traditional confines:

> *"Sleep is the best meditation." - Dalai Lama*

Quotes from modern thinkers reflect a growing appreciation for the intricate interplay between sleep and mental health, underscoring the holistic nature of well-being.

The Sleep Cycle

The sleep cycle, a fundamental aspect of human biology, has been a subject of fascination and study for centuries. From ancient civilizations to the contemporary digital age, the understanding and significance of the sleep cycle have evolved. Let us explore the historical perspectives, contemporary definitions, and the challenges posed by the modern lifestyle, particularly the impact of screen time on the sleep cycle.

Historical Perspectives:

Ancient Beliefs and Practices: In ancient cultures, sleep was often associated with spiritual experiences and considered a bridge between the earthly and divine realms. The Greeks, for instance, believed in Hypnos, the god of sleep, while the Egyptians associated sleep with the journey to the afterlife. Practices such as dream interpretation were prevalent in societies like Babylon and Mesopotamia.

Medieval and Renaissance Views:

During the medieval and Renaissance periods, sleep was often linked to humoral theories of health. The works of prominent figures like Hippocrates and Galen emphasized the importance of balance in bodily fluids for a sound sleep cycle. Sleep was considered essential for maintaining overall well-being.

Scientific Understanding:

With advancements in neuroscience and sleep research, the 20th century witnessed a paradigm shift in the understanding of the sleep cycle. The sleep cycle, consisting of multiple stages, plays a crucial role in memory consolidation, immune function, and emotional regulation.

Chronobiology and Circadian Rhythms:

Modern definitions of the sleep cycle incorporate the principles of chronobiology, which studies biological rhythms. Circadian rhythms, regulated by the internal biological clock, influence the sleep-wake cycle. Understanding these natural rhythms is crucial for optimizing sleep quality and overall health.

Screen Time and Blue Light Exposure:

As researchers explore further into the effects of blue light, studies suggest its role in delaying sleep onset and reducing overall sleep quality. Strategies such as using blue light filters or adjusting screen settings aim to mitigate these effects, emphasizing the importance of managing technology use for better sleep hygiene. Despite these challenges, technology also offers innovations like sleep-tracking apps and relaxation aids that seek to enhance sleep patterns in our modern, interconnected world.

Social and Work Pressures:

Modern lifestyles, characterized by hectic work schedules and social pressures, often lead to sleep deprivation. The constant connectivity through digital devices blurs the lines between work and personal life, making it challenging for individuals to establish a consistent sleep routine.

Impact of Screen Time on Adolescents:

Numerous studies have highlighted the adverse effects of excessive screen time on adolescents' sleep patterns. The American Academy of Pediatrics recommends limiting screen time for children and adolescents, as the exposure to screens before bedtime can lead to delayed sleep onset and shortened sleep duration.

Workplace Challenges:

Case studies in corporate environments reveal the negative impact of irregular work hours and constant connectivity on employees' sleep cycles. The prevalence of remote work, while providing flexibility, has also blurred the boundaries between professional and personal life, contributing to sleep disturbances.

"Arianna Huffington:

We sacrifice sleep in the name of productivity, but ironically, our loss of sleep, despite the extra hours we put in at work, adds up to more than eleven days of lost productivity per year per worker."

Matthew Walker:

The shorter your sleep, the shorter your life. The leading causes of disease and death in developed nations—diseases that are crippling health-care systems, such as heart disease, obesity, dementia, diabetes, and cancer—all have recognized causal links to a lack of sleep.

CHAPTER II

The Importance of Sleep

In 1965, a 17-year-old high school student named Randy Gardner decided to conduct an experiment for a science fair: he wanted to break the world record for the longest time awake. He managed to stay awake for 11 days and 25 minutes, setting a new record. However, the effects on his body and mind were severe, highlighting the critical importance of sleep.

Initially, Randy experienced mood changes, irritability, and trouble concentrating. As the days went on, his cognitive abilities deteriorated further. He struggled with short-term memory and had trouble focusing on simple tasks. By day four, he started to experience hallucinations and paranoia. His speech became slurred, and his ability to form coherent thoughts diminished.

After completing the experiment, Randy slept for 14 hours straight, but it took several weeks for his body and mind to fully recover. This extreme case demonstrated the essential role of sleep in maintaining mental and physical health. Chronic sleep deprivation, even at lower levels, can lead to serious issues such as impaired cognitive function, weakened immune system, increased stress, and higher risk of chronic conditions like heart disease and diabetes.

Randy's story serves as a powerful reminder of why sleep is not just a luxury but a vital component of overall well-being.

Physical Health Benefits of Sleep

Immune System Support

Sleep is crucial for maintaining a healthy immune system. During sleep, the body produces cytokines, proteins that aid in fighting infections and inflammation. Lack of sleep can reduce the production of these protective cytokines, making the body more susceptible to infections and illnesses. Chronic sleep deprivation can also weaken the immune system's response to vaccines, diminishing their effectiveness. Ensuring adequate sleep strengthens the body's ability to combat infections, heal wounds, and recover from illnesses.

"*"Six months no beer. Kinda dumb to post this, but I'm proud of my hard work and so are my trainers... Physical fitness feels good. #GOTG"*

- Chris Pratt"

The Story of Chris Pratt

Weight Management

Chris Pratt initially gained fame for his role as Andy Dwyer on the television series "Parks and Recreation." His character was known for being lovable but out of shape, which reflected Pratt's physical condition at the time. He often joked about his weight and embraced his heavier physique, but his health and self-image were impacted.

In 2013, Pratt was cast as Peter Quill/Star-Lord in Marvel's "Guardians of the Galaxy." This role required a significant physical transformation, pushing Pratt to adopt a rigorous fitness and nutrition regimen. Over the course of six months, he lost about 60 pounds through a combination of intensive workouts and a strict diet.

Pratt's diet included nutrient-dense foods and cut out processed sugars, unhealthy fats, and refined carbohydrates. He focused on lean proteins, vegetables, fruits, and whole grains. His workout routine, guided by a professional trainer, included a mix of cardio, weightlifting, and high-intensity interval training (HIIT). He also engaged in activities like swimming, boxing, and mountain biking to keep his workouts varied and enjoyable.

The transformation was remarkable not just in terms of physical appearance but also in Pratt's overall health and well-being. He reported feeling more energetic, confident, and happier. His successful weight management not only prepared him for the demanding role in "Guardians of the Galaxy" but also set a new standard for his future roles, including in "Jurassic World" and "Avengers: Endgame."

Pratt's journey underscores the importance of a balanced diet and consistent exercise, but it also highlights the significance of motivation and professional guidance. His story is a testament to how dedication and hard work can lead to significant and lasting health improvements, inspiring many fans and individuals striving for similar goals.

Chris Pratt's weight management journey also underscores the importance of sleep in achieving fitness and health goals. While diet and exercise are often highlighted in weight loss stories, Pratt has spoken about how getting enough quality sleep was a crucial component of his transformation.

During his weight loss journey, Pratt ensured he got sufficient sleep each night. Adequate sleep helps regulate the hormones ghrelin and leptin, which control hunger and appetite. Ghrelin stimulates appetite, while leptin signals to the brain when you're full. Lack of sleep can disrupt this balance, leading to increased hunger and cravings for high-calorie foods. By prioritizing sleep, Pratt was able to better control his appetite and make healthier food choices.

Sleep plays a significant role in regulating hormones that control hunger and appetite, such as ghrelin and leptin. Ghrelin stimulates appetite, while leptin signals fullness to the brain. When sleep-deprived, the body produces more ghrelin and less leptin, leading to increased hunger and appetite, often resulting in overeating and weight gain. Additionally, lack of sleep can lead to increased cravings for high-calorie, carbohydrate-rich foods. Chronic sleep deprivation disrupts the body's metabolic processes, further contributing to weight gain. By getting sufficient sleep, individuals can better manage their weight, reduce the risk of obesity, and maintain a healthier lifestyle. Furthermore, adequate sleep supports overall metabolic health and enhances the body's ability to regulate energy balance effectively.

Cardiovascular Health

Quality sleep is crucial for maintaining optimal cardiovascular health. While sleeping, the body engages in vital processes that promote the repair and rejuvenation of the cardiovascular system. Adequate sleep supports the regulation of blood pressure, inflammation reduction, and maintenance of a healthy heart rate. Chronic sleep deprivation, on the other hand, is linked to a heightened risk of hypertension, heart disease, heart attacks, and strokes. Moreover, insufficient sleep can contribute to the accumulation of arterial plaques, thereby exacerbating cardiovascular risks. Making sleep a priority can greatly enhance long-term cardiovascular well-being and mitigate the likelihood of heart-related ailments.

Mental Health Benefits of Sleep

Emotional Regulation

Quality sleep plays a vital role in emotional regulation. During sleep, especially REM (Rapid Eye Movement) sleep, the brain processes and consolidates emotions and experiences from the day. This helps maintain emotional stability and resilience. When we are sleep-deprived, the brain's ability to regulate emotions is impaired, leading to increased irritability, mood swings, and heightened emotional responses. Adequate sleep helps us manage our emotions better, enabling us to respond to situations more calmly and rationally.

For instance, during his weight management journey, Chris Pratt emphasized the importance of sleep in maintaining a positive outlook and emotional stability. The intense physical training and dietary changes could have been mentally taxing, but by ensuring sufficient sleep, Pratt could keep his emotions in check and stay motivated.

Stress Reduction

Sleep is a natural stress reliever. When we sleep, our body reduces the levels of stress hormones like cortisol. Chronic sleep deprivation can lead to elevated cortisol levels, which can increase stress and anxiety. Moreover, lack of sleep can make it more challenging to cope with stressors, exacerbating feelings of stress and anxiety. By getting enough rest, we can lower stress levels, improve our mood, and enhance our ability to deal with daily challenges.

Cognitive Function

Sleep is essential for cognitive functions such as memory, learning, problem-solving, and decision-making. During sleep, the brain consolidates new information and strengthens neural connections, which is crucial for learning and memory retention. Sleep deprivation can impair cognitive functions, leading to difficulties in concentration, decision-making, and problem-solving.

CHAPTER III

Understanding Sleep Cycles

Understanding the intricacies of sleep involves exploring the distinct stages such as REM (Rapid Eye Movement) and Non-REM (Non-Rapid Eye Movement), each playing crucial roles in our nightly restorative processes. Additionally, grasping the influence of circadian rhythms and the biological clock elucidates how our bodies naturally regulate sleep-wake cycles. By comprehending these fundamental aspects of sleep physiology, individuals can gain valuable insights into optimizing their sleep patterns to enhance both quality of sleep and overall health.

Overview of Sleep Stages

Sleep is divided into two main types: Non-REM sleep and REM sleep. Each type has distinct characteristics and plays a unique role in maintaining our health.

Non-REM Sleep

Non-REM sleep is further divided into three stages:

1. **Stage 1 (N1):** This is the lightest stage of sleep, where you drift in and out of sleep and can be awakened easily. It typically lasts a few minutes and involves slow eye movements and muscle relaxation. Some people may experience sudden muscle contractions, often preceded by a sensation of falling.
2. **Stage 2 (N2):** This stage is characterized by a slightly deeper sleep. Eye movements stop, and brain waves slow down with occasional bursts of rapid activity known as sleep spindles and K-complexes. This stage accounts for about 50% of the total sleep cycle.
3. **Stage 3 (N3):** Also known as deep sleep or slow-wave sleep, this stage is the most restorative. During this stage, the brain produces delta waves, and it becomes harder to wake up. Deep sleep is crucial for physical recovery, growth, and immune system functioning.

REM Sleep

REM sleep is a unique stage characterized by rapid eye movements, increased brain activity, and vivid dreams. It typically occurs about 90 minutes after falling asleep and recurs multiple times throughout the night, with each REM period becoming longer. During REM sleep, the body is temporarily paralyzed, which prevents acting out dreams. This stage is vital for cognitive functions such as memory consolidation, learning, and emotional regulation.

Circadian Rhythms and the Biological Clock

Our sleep patterns are regulated by circadian rhythms, which are natural, internal processes that follow a roughly 24-hour cycle. These rhythms influence various bodily functions, including the sleep-wake cycle, hormone release, and body temperature.

The Biological Clock

At the heart of circadian rhythms is the biological clock, a group of nerve cells in the brain known as the suprachiasmatic nucleus (SCN), located in the hypothalamus. The SCN receives information about light exposure from the eyes and uses this information to coordinate the timing of various physiological processes, including sleep.

Influence of Light

Light plays a pivotal role in regulating circadian rhythms, serving as the primary external cue. Exposure to natural light during daylight hours helps synchronize our internal body clocks with the external environment. On the other hand, exposure to artificial light, particularly blue light emitted by screens, can disrupt these rhythms and adversely impact the quality of sleep. Therefore, it is advisable to limit screen time before bedtime to promote optimal sleep hygiene. Ensuring adequate exposure to natural light during the day and minimizing artificial light exposure at night are crucial strategies for maintaining healthy circadian rhythms and improving overall sleep quality.

Disruptions to Circadian Rhythms

Disruptions to circadian rhythms can lead to sleep disorders and other health issues. Common factors that can disrupt these rhythms include:

- **Shift Work:** Working irregular hours or night shifts can interfere with the natural sleep-wake cycle.
- **Jet Lag:** Traveling across time zones can temporarily misalign the biological clock with the local time.
- **Lifestyle Factors:** Irregular sleep schedules, lack of exposure to natural light, and excessive use of electronic devices can all disrupt circadian rhythms.

By understanding the stages of sleep, the role of REM and Non-REM sleep, and the importance of circadian rhythms and the biological clock, you can take steps to improve your sleep quality and overall health.

CHAPTER IV

The Science of Sleep

Sleep is a fascinating, complex, and vital part of our daily lives. As Arianna Huffington once said, "

"Sleep is a performance-enhancing wonder drug. The more you sleep, the better you live, the longer you live, and the more creative you become."

Brain Activity During Sleep

Imagine you're standing in front of a grand concert hall. The lights dim, and the symphony begins to play, each instrument harmonizing to create a beautiful piece of music. This is similar to what happens in our brains during sleep. While our bodies rest, our brains are anything but idle.

During sleep, especially in the REM (Rapid Eye Movement) stage, brain activity increases to levels similar to when we're awake. This phase is crucial for memory consolidation, learning, and emotional regulation. The brain goes through different sleep cycles, including REM and non-REM sleep, each playing a unique role. Non-REM sleep, particularly the deep sleep stages, is essential for physical restoration and energy conservation.

Neuroscientist Matthew Walker explains,

"When we're in deep sleep, a process called synaptic pruning takes place. The brain clears out unnecessary connections, making room for new learning and memory formation."

This pruning is essential for cognitive function and overall mental health.

Hormones and Sleep Regulation

Sleep is regulated by a delicate balance of hormones. Have you ever felt sleepy at the same time every night or found it hard to wake up in the morning? This is due to the circadian rhythm, our internal body clock, which is influenced by the hormone melatonin. Produced by the pineal gland in response to darkness, melatonin signals the body that it's time to wind down and prepare for sleep.

Cortisol, often known as the stress hormone, also plays a role. Levels of cortisol decrease as melatonin rises, promoting a state of relaxation conducive to sleep. However, elevated cortisol levels due to stress or irregular sleep patterns can disrupt this balance, leading to sleep disturbances.

As Dr. Michael Breus, a clinical psychologist and sleep specialist, puts it,

""Hormones are the conductors of our sleep orchestra. When they are in harmony, the music of sleep is beautiful. When they are out of sync, the entire symphony can fall apart.""

Sleep Disorders and Their Impact

Sleep disorders are more common than many realize and can have profound effects on our health and well-being. Insomnia, sleep apnea, restless legs syndrome, and narcolepsy are some of the most prevalent sleep disorders. Insomnia, characterized by difficulty falling or staying asleep, can be triggered by stress, anxiety, or poor sleep habits. Sleep apnea, where breathing repeatedly stops and starts during sleep, can lead to severe cardiovascular problems if left untreated.

Michael Phelps, born in 1985, is considered one of the greatest athletes of all time. His journey to becoming the most decorated Olympian in history is both inspiring and revealing of the challenges elite athletes face.

Phelps started swimming at a young age, initially to burn off energy and manage his ADHD. His talent in the pool was apparent early on, and by the age of 15, he made his Olympic debut at the 2000 Sydney Games, becoming the youngest male to make a U.S. Olympic swim team in 68 years. Although he didn't win a medal in Sydney, the experience fueled his determination.

Over the next several years, Phelps dominated the sport. At the 2004 Athens Olympics, he won six gold and two bronze medals. He then went on to achieve a historic feat at the 2008 Beijing Olympics, winning eight gold medals and breaking Mark Spitz's 1972 record of seven gold medals in a single Games.

However, behind the scenes, Phelps struggled with his mental health. The pressure to maintain his performance, along with the physical and emotional demands of being at the top of his sport, took a significant toll. After the 2012 London Olympics, where he won four gold and two silver medals, Phelps retired, feeling burnt out and lost.

In the years following his initial retirement, Phelps faced severe depression and anxiety. He felt disconnected from the world outside the pool and struggled with finding his identity beyond swimming. His mental health issues culminated in a DUI arrest in 2014, which led him to seek help.

Phelps entered a treatment program and began working on his mental health. He spoke openly about his struggles with depression and the importance of seeking help, becoming an advocate for mental health awareness. His honesty helped to reduce the stigma around mental health issues, particularly among athletes.

Remarkably, Phelps returned to competitive swimming and made a triumphant comeback at the 2016 Rio Olympics. He added five gold and one silver medal to his collection, bringing his total Olympic medal count to 28, including 23 golds. His performance in Rio was not just a testament to his physical prowess but also to his resilience and determination to overcome his personal battles.

Today, Michael Phelps continues to be a prominent advocate for mental health, sharing his story to inspire others to seek help and prioritize their well-being.

The impact of sleep disorders extends beyond physical health. They can affect cognitive function, emotional stability, and overall quality of life. As Dr. William Dement, a pioneer in sleep medicine, famously said,

""Healthy sleep has been empirically proven to be the single most important determinant in predicting longevity, more influential than diet, exercise, or genetics.""

CHAPTER V

The Sleep Sashtra

""True harmony within our dwellings creates tranquility within our hearts. In the balance of our surroundings, we find the rest our souls seek and the strength to lead with wisdom and compassion."*
— Maharaja Vikramaditya"*

The Sleepless King: A Tale of Vastu Shastra

Once upon a time, in ancient India, there was a renowned king named Maharaja Vikramaditya, who ruled over a prosperous kingdom. Maharaja Vikramaditya was known for his wisdom, bravery, and just rule. His kingdom flourished under his leadership, and his people adored him. However, despite his success and the peace in his realm, the king struggled with a severe case of insomnia.

For many months, Maharaja Vikramaditya found himself unable to sleep through the night. He would toss and turn in his grand palace, his mind racing with thoughts, and his body weary but unable to rest. His lack of sleep began to affect his ability to govern, and he became irritable and distracted. His advisors and ministers grew worried, as did the people of the kingdom, for they could see their beloved king's suffering.

Desperate for a solution, Maharaja Vikramaditya sought the advice of the wisest scholars, doctors, and sages from across the land. They tried various remedies, from herbal concoctions to meditation practices, but nothing seemed to work. One day, a renowned Vastu Shastra expert named Acharya Vaidyanath arrived at the palace, offering his services to the king.

Acharya Vaidyanath was a revered figure known for his deep understanding of Vastu Shastra, the ancient Indian science of architecture. He believed that the king's insomnia could be related to the energy flow within the palace itself. With the king's permission, Acharya Vaidyanath conducted a thorough analysis of the palace's layout, orientation, and design.

After careful examination, Acharya Vaidyanath identified several Vastu Shastra-related issues in the king's bedroom:

Bedroom Location: The king's bedroom was located in the north-east corner of the palace, a direction associated with growth and new beginnings but not ideal for restful sleep. The recommended location for a master bedroom was the south-west corner, which symbolizes stability and peace.

Bed Placement: The king's bed was positioned with his head facing north, a direction considered unfavorable for sleep. According to Vastu Shastra, sleeping with the head towards the south promotes health and longevity, while the east direction enhances relaxation and mental clarity.

Clutter and Decor: The king's bedroom was adorned with numerous artifacts, weapons, and mirrors, creating a chaotic environment that disrupted the flow of positive energy. Acharya Vaidyanath advised removing unnecessary items and replacing them with calming elements like soft drapes and soothing colors.

Ventilation and Lighting: The bedroom lacked proper ventilation and had heavy curtains that blocked natural light during the day. Acharya Vaidyanath recommended improving air circulation and allowing natural light to enter during the daytime while using light-blocking curtains at night to ensure darkness.

With the king's approval, Acharya Vaidyanath and his team made the necessary changes to the bedroom according to Vastu Shastra principles. The bedroom was relocated to the south-west corner of the palace, the bed was repositioned with the head facing south, and the room was decluttered and redecorated with calming elements. Proper ventilation was ensured, and the lighting was adjusted to support the king's natural sleep cycle.

Within a few days of these changes, Maharaja Vikramaditya began to experience a significant improvement in his sleep. He found himself falling asleep more easily, and his nights became restful and rejuvenating. As his sleep improved, so did his mood and energy levels. The king's ability to govern was restored, and the entire kingdom rejoiced at the return of their well-rested and vibrant ruler.

Maharaja Vikramaditya, grateful for Acharya Vaidyanath's wisdom, became an ardent supporter of Vastu Shastra. He ensured that the principles were applied not only in his palace but also throughout the kingdom, believing that the harmony between humans and their environment was essential for a prosperous and peaceful life.

The Sleep Sashtra

In Vastu Shastra, the ancient Indian science of architecture, the orientation and arrangement of spaces within a home are believed to significantly influence various aspects of life, including sleep. According to Vastu principles, the proper alignment and design of a bedroom can promote restful sleep and overall well-being. Here's how sleep is related to Vastu Shastra which we can now on call as **"The Sleep Sashtra"**.

1. Bedroom Location

South-West Corner: The ideal location for the master bedroom is the south-west corner of the house. This direction is associated with stability and security, which can help promote sound sleep.

North-West Corner: This direction is suitable for guest bedrooms or children's bedrooms. It is believed to be good for relaxation and rest.

2. Bed Placement

Head Direction: When sleeping, it is recommended to place the head towards the south or east. Sleeping with the head towards the south is thought to enhance health and longevity, while sleeping with the head towards the east is believed to improve memory and concentration.

Bed Position: The bed should be placed away from the walls, preferably with the headboard against a solid wall. It should not be directly in line with the door or under a window, as this can disrupt the flow of positive energy (prana) and affect sleep.

3. Bedroom Shape and Layout

Shape: The bedroom should be square or rectangular in shape to ensure a balanced flow of energy. Irregularly shaped rooms can cause restlessness and disturbed sleep.

Clutter-Free: Keeping the bedroom tidy and free of clutter is important, as clutter can obstruct the flow of energy and create stress, impacting sleep quality.

4. Colors and Decor

Colors: Soft, soothing colors such as light blue, green, and lavender are recommended for the bedroom, as they promote calmness and relaxation.

Decor: Avoid placing mirrors directly facing the bed, as they are believed to disrupt sleep and cause restlessness. Also, avoid placing electronic devices and work-related items in the bedroom to create a serene and restful environment.

5. Lighting and Ventilation

Natural Light: Ensure that the bedroom receives adequate natural light during the day to maintain a healthy circadian rhythm. However, use curtains or blinds to block out excessive light at night.

Ventilation: Good ventilation is essential for maintaining a fresh and healthy environment in the bedroom. Proper air circulation can contribute to better sleep quality.

6. Energy Flow

Positive Energy: The arrangement and orientation of furniture and objects in the bedroom should allow for a smooth flow of positive energy. Avoid sharp corners and heavy beams directly above the bed, as they can create negative energy and disturb sleep.

As Maharaja Vikramaditya discovered, the harmony within our dwellings profoundly impacts the tranquility within our hearts. By aligning his surroundings according to Vastu Shastra principles, he found the restful sleep he so desperately needed, which in turn restored his strength and ability to lead with wisdom and compassion. This tale reminds us that the balance of our environment not only shapes our physical well-being but also nurtures our inner peace and fortitude. Just as the king's journey to restful nights brought harmony to his reign, may we all seek such balance in our lives, finding the tranquility and strength to face each day with renewed vigor.

CHAPTER VI

Sleep and Productivity

""Sleep is the best meditation. A good night's sleep is the foundation for a productive day ahead." — Dalai Lama"

During sleep, the brain undergoes a process known as synaptic pruning, which is crucial for maintaining cognitive function and overall brain health. This process involves the elimination of weaker synaptic connections to make room for the strengthening of more useful ones.

Number of Synapses: The human brain contains roughly 100 trillion synapses, which are the connections between neurons that allow for communication within the brain.

Daily Pruning: Every night, during sleep, the brain can prune up to 20% of its synapses. This pruning helps remove unnecessary or weak connections, improving the efficiency and performance of neural networks.

Energy Efficiency: Synaptic pruning conserves energy and resources, ensuring that the brain can function optimally during wakefulness.

This process is particularly intense during REM sleep, a stage characterized by vivid dreaming and high brain activity. Synaptic pruning is essential for learning, memory consolidation, and overall cognitive health, making sleep an indispensable component of brain function and productivity.

The Link Between Sleep and Performance

Sleep is intricately linked to performance across various domains, including cognitive, emotional, and physical functions. Here are some interesting facts and figures highlighting this connection.

Productivity Loss

Sleep deprivation costs the U.S. economy an estimated $411 billion annually in lost productivity, according to a study by RAND Corporation.

Athletic Performance

Studies show that athletes who get adequate sleep (typically 8-10 hours) have faster reaction times, better accuracy, and improved speed compared to sleep-deprived athletes.

Workplace Performance

Employees who sleep poorly are more likely to experience decreased concentration, memory lapses, and difficulty making decisions, all of which impact their productivity and performance at work.

Safety Concerns

Sleep-deprived individuals are more prone to accidents and errors. For instance, drowsy driving is responsible for an estimated 1,550 fatalities and 40,000 nonfatal injuries annually in the United States alone.

Sleep's Impact on Cognitive Abilities

Sleep plays a crucial role in enhancing cognitive abilities and maintaining brain health. Adequate sleep supports neuroplasticity, the brain's ability to adapt and reorganize itself. Here are some compelling facts and figures related to this impact.

Memory Consolidation

During sleep, especially REM sleep, the brain consolidates memories from short-term to long-term storage. This process is essential for learning and retaining new information, and disruptions in sleep can significantly impair memory retention.

Creativity and Problem-Solving

Studies have found that sleep enhances creative thinking and problem-solving skills. During sleep, the brain reorganizes and restructures information, leading to novel insights and solutions, and helping individuals approach problems with fresh perspectives.

Emotional Regulation

Adequate sleep supports emotional resilience and regulation. Sleep-deprived individuals are more susceptible to mood swings, irritability, and stress, which can impair cognitive function.

Neurological Health

Chronic sleep deprivation is associated with an increased risk of neurodegenerative diseases such as Alzheimer's and Parkinson's disease. Sleep is crucial for clearing out toxins and maintaining brain health.

CHAPTER VII

Sleep Hygiene

Daphne's Dance of Vigilant Slumber: The Dolphin's Tale of Sleep Hygiene

In the vast expanse of the ocean, where the sun's rays dance upon the waves and the depths hide mysteries untold, there lives a creature known for its grace and intelligence: the dolphin.

Meet Daphne, a bottlenose dolphin with a shimmering silver-gray coat that glints in the sunlight. Daphne is not just any dolphin—she's a master of sleep hygiene, a trait crucial for survival in the unpredictable waters she calls home.

You see, Daphne's day begins with a lively dance through the waves, chasing schools of shimmering fish with her pod. But as the sun starts to dip beneath the horizon, signaling the approach of night, Daphne knows it's time to settle in for rest.

Unlike many land-dwelling creatures who curl up in cozy nests, Daphne and her podmates have a unique way of sleeping. They practice unihemispheric slow-wave sleep—a fancy term that means one half of their brain rests while the other stays awake and alert. This remarkable adaptation allows them to drift into slumber while still keeping an eye out for lurking predators or unexpected visitors in their watery world.

Throughout the night, Daphne takes turns with her podmates, ensuring that everyone gets the rest they need without ever fully letting their guard down. This way, they maintain their safety while navigating the dark, mysterious depths beneath the moonlit surface.

Despite the challenges of ocean life, Daphne's method ensures she remains vigilant and healthy. This careful balance of rest and alertness showcases the incredible adaptability of dolphins in their natural habitat.

Come morning, as the first rays of sunlight paint the ocean in hues of gold and pink, Daphne emerges from her night of vigilant rest. Refreshed and ready, she rejoins her pod, ready to explore, play, and hunt once more.

Optimizing Your Sleep Environment: The Key to Better Rest

Sleep is essential for our physical and mental well-being, yet many struggle to achieve quality rest. One often-overlooked factor in this struggle is our sleep environment. Creating a conducive atmosphere can significantly enhance our ability to fall asleep and stay asleep. Here's how you can transform your bedroom into a sleep-inducing sanctuary.

1. Lighting and Ambiance:

Dim the Lights: In the evening, reduce bright overhead lights and opt for softer, warmer lighting. Consider using lamps with adjustable brightness or dimmer switches to create a calming atmosphere conducive to sleep. You might use a bedside lamp with a dimmer switch to create a relaxing atmosphere conducive to sleep.

Blue Light Filters: Minimize exposure to blue light from screens (phones, tablets, computers) as it can interfere with melatonin production, which regulates sleep. Use apps or screen filters that reduce blue light emission in the hours before bedtime to signal to your body that it's time to wind down. Install apps like Flux or use built-in settings on devices such as iPhones and Androids that automatically reduce blue light emission as bedtime approaches. This helps maintain melatonin production, promoting better sleep quality.

2. Comfortable Bedding:

Mattress and Pillows: Invest in a high-quality mattress and pillows that provide adequate support and comfort for your sleeping position. Mattresses should be replaced every 7-10 years, and pillows should be swapped out every 1-2 years, depending on wear and tear. A good mattress and pillow combination can help alleviate aches and pains, contributing to a more restful night's sleep. Additionally, regularly cleaning and maintaining your bedding can prolong its life and enhance sleep hygiene.

Temperature Control: Keep your bedroom cool, ideally between 60-67°F (15-19°C). A cooler environment tends to promote better sleep as it mimics the body's natural temperature drop during sleep. Using breathable, moisture-wicking bedding can further enhance comfort in maintaining an optimal sleep temperature. Adjusting your thermostat or using a fan can help regulate your room's temperature to create the perfect sleeping environment.

3. Noise and Disturbances:

Soundproofing: Minimize external noises using earplugs, white noise machines, or soundproofing materials if you live in a noisy area. White noise machines can create a constant, soothing sound that masks disruptive noises and promotes deeper sleep. Earplugs like Mack's Ultra Soft Foam Earplugs or a white noise machine like LectroFan can also be tried. Alternatively, use soundproof curtains or acoustic panels to dampen outside noise.

Peaceful Atmosphere: Establish a relaxing bedtime routine that signals to your body it's time to unwind. This could include reading a book, practicing relaxation techniques such as deep breathing or progressive muscle relaxation, or taking a warm bath with calming essential oils like lavender.

The Role of Technology in Sleep

Technology can both hinder and help our sleep patterns. While screens emit blue light that disrupts our natural sleep-wake cycles, certain technologies can aid in establishing healthier sleep habits:

Sleep Tracking Devices: Wearable gadgets and apps can monitor your sleep patterns, providing insights into your sleep quality and helping you identify areas for improvement. They can track factors like sleep duration, sleep stages, and interruptions, helping you make informed adjustments to your sleep environment and habits.

Smart Home Devices: Use smart lighting systems that mimic natural light patterns to regulate your circadian rhythm. Some can be programmed to dim gradually in the evening, signaling to your body that it's time to wind down and prepare for sleep. Additionally, smart thermostats can help maintain a comfortable bedroom temperature throughout the night.

Apps for Relaxation: Consider meditation or white noise apps that can help you relax and drift off to sleep more easily. These apps often offer guided meditations, calming music, or nature sounds that promote relaxation and reduce stress levels before bedtime.

Establishing a Consistent Sleep Schedule

Maintaining a regular sleep schedule is vital for optimizing sleep quality and overall health. Here are practical tips to achieve a consistent routine:

Set a Bedtime: Aim to go to bed and wake up at the same time every day, even on weekends. Consistency reinforces your body's natural sleep-wake cycle, making it easier to fall asleep and wake up refreshed.

Limit Naps: If you nap during the day, keep it short (20-30 minutes) and avoid napping late in the afternoon, as this can interfere with nighttime sleep.

Avoid Stimulants: Limit caffeine and nicotine intake, especially in the hours leading up to bedtime. Both are stimulants that can disrupt sleep patterns and make it harder to fall asleep.

Wind Down: Establish a relaxing bedtime routine that signals to your body it's time to sleep. This could include reading a book, taking a warm bath, practicing gentle yoga or stretching exercises, or listening to calming music. Avoid screens and stimulating activities close to bedtime, as they can interfere with your ability to relax and fall asleep.

By prioritizing your sleep environment, leveraging technology wisely, and sticking to a consistent sleep schedule, you can significantly enhance your sleep quality and overall well-being.

CHAPTER VIII

Sleep Across the Lifespan

The Giant Who Slept

In the ancient Indian epic, the Ramayana, Kumbakarna is a figure both awe-inspiring and tragic. He was a giant, the younger brother of the demon king Ravana, and renowned for his incredible strength. However, what made Kumbakarna truly unique was his extraordinary sleep cycle.

Kumbakarna's tale of sleep began with an act of devotion. He, along with his brothers Ravana and Vibhishana, performed intense penance to please Lord Brahma, seeking boons to make them invincible. When Brahma appeared to grant their wishes, Kumbakarna intended to ask for Indraasana (the throne of Indra, king of the gods). However, due to divine intervention by the goddess Saraswati, who was requested by Indra to prevent Kumbakarna from becoming too powerful, he instead asked for Nidraasana (the bed of sleep).

Realizing the potential devastation Kumbakarna could cause if he were constantly awake, Brahma granted him a modified boon: Kumbakarna would sleep for six months at a stretch and be awake for only one day before falling back into deep slumber. This curse-turned-boon had a profound impact on Kumbakarna's life and legacy.

During his periods of sleep, Kumbakarna was completely oblivious to the world around him. His deep slumber was so profound that it took an enormous effort to wake him. His family and soldiers would use loud noises, pricking, and even elephants walking over him to rouse him from his sleep when needed.

When Kumbakarna was awake, his hunger and strength were insatiable. He would consume vast quantities of food and drink, displaying his formidable power. Despite his limited waking hours, Kumbakarna remained fiercely loyal to his brother Ravana and the kingdom of Lanka.

The significance of Kumbakarna's sleep came to the forefront during the great war between Rama and Ravana. As Ravana's forces struggled against Rama's divine army, Ravana decided to wake Kumbakarna to turn the tide of battle. It took great effort and many soldiers to awaken the sleeping giant. When he finally awoke, he was informed of the dire situation and immediately prepared for battle, despite knowing the righteousness of Rama's cause.

Kumbakarna's short period of wakefulness was marked by his towering presence on the battlefield. His immense strength and ferocity caused great destruction among Rama's troops. However, his power was ultimately no match for the divine warriors, and he was slain by Rama after a fierce battle.

Kumbakarna's story highlights the critical role of sleep, even for the mightiest of beings. His deep and prolonged sleep was both a curse and a necessity, shaping his actions and fate. It serves as a reminder of the importance of sleep in maintaining balance and strength, and how even the strongest individuals are bound by the natural need for rest.

Kumbakarna's tale is a fascinating blend of myth and morality, illustrating how sleep, often overlooked, is a fundamental part of life that influences our capabilities and destiny.

Sleep Like a Baby?

The phrase "sleep like a baby" might make one think of peaceful, uninterrupted sleep. However, infants have unique sleep patterns. Newborns sleep for about 14-17 hours a day but wake up frequently due to their need for feeding, comfort, and diaper changes. Infants spend around 50% of their sleep time in Rapid Eye Movement (REM) sleep, which is crucial for brain development. In comparison, adults spend only about 20-25% of their sleep in REM. This high proportion of REM sleep helps infants process the massive amount of new information they encounter daily. But interestingly a lion cub, for instance, can sleep up to 20 hours a day, while a newborn giraffe might only sleep for about 30 minutes to an hour in short intervals.

Sleep in Infants and Children

Sleep Duration:

- Infants (0-3 months): Need about 14-17 hours of sleep per day.
- Infants (4-11 months): Need about 12-15 hours of sleep per day.
- Toddlers (1-2 years): Require 11-14 hours of sleep per day.
- Preschoolers (3-5 years): Need around 10-13 hours of sleep per day.

- School-age children (6-13 years): Require 9-11 hours of sleep per day.

Newborns require a significant amount of sleep, typically around 14-17 hours each day. Their sleep is split into multiple short periods because they need to wake frequently for feeding. This stage of sleep is crucial for brain development and physical growth.

- Establish a routine, even if it's simple, to signal sleep time.
- Ensure the sleep environment is safe and comfortable.
- Watch for signs of sleepiness to avoid overtiredness.

As infants grow, their sleep needs decrease slightly to about 12-15 hours per day. Most infants at this age start sleeping longer stretches at night and take 2-3 naps during the day. Developing a bedtime routine can be beneficial.

- Introduce a consistent bedtime routine, like a bath followed by reading.
- Encourage self-soothing by putting the baby to bed while drowsy but awake.
- Maintain a consistent sleep schedule, even on weekends.

Toddlers need around 11-14 hours of sleep per day, which typically includes one nap. A regular sleep schedule is crucial for this age group, as it helps regulate their internal body clock.

- Keep bedtime and naptime routines consistent.
- Create a calming pre-sleep routine.
- Avoid stimulating activities close to bedtime.

Preschoolers need about 10-13 hours of sleep each day. Most children in this age group will transition from napping during the day to sleeping longer at night.

- Maintain a regular sleep schedule.
- Make the sleep environment quiet and dark.
- Limit screen time before bed to help them wind down.

School-age children require 9-11 hours of sleep per night. Adequate sleep is crucial for their academic performance, emotional stability, and overall health.

- Encourage a regular bedtime, even on weekends.
- Ensure they have a sleep-friendly environment, free of distractions.
- Foster healthy sleep habits, such as reading before bed instead of using electronic devices.

Sleep Challenges in Adolescents

Adolescence is a period of significant physical, emotional, and cognitive development, and adequate sleep is essential during this time. However, adolescents often face unique sleep challenges that can impact their overall health and well-being.

1. Biological Changes:

Circadian Rhythm Shift: During adolescence, there is a natural shift in the circadian rhythm, leading to a preference for later bedtimes and wake times. This shift is due to hormonal changes that delay the release of melatonin, the sleep hormone.

Sleep Phase Delay: This shift often results in a condition known as delayed sleep phase syndrome, where teenagers have difficulty falling asleep early and prefer to wake up later in the morning.

2. Lifestyle Factors:

Academic Pressure: Increased academic demands, homework, extracurricular activities, and early school start times can contribute to sleep deprivation.

Social Activities: Adolescents often prioritize socializing, both in person and online, over sleep, leading to late bedtimes.

Technology Use: The use of electronic devices such as smartphones, tablets, and computers before bedtime can interfere with sleep. The blue light emitted by screens suppresses melatonin production, making it harder to fall asleep.

3. Psychological Factors:

Stress and Anxiety: Adolescents are susceptible to stress and anxiety related to academics, social relationships, and future prospects. These factors can contribute to difficulty falling and staying asleep.

Mental Health Issues: Conditions such as depression and anxiety can negatively impact sleep patterns.

Sleep Considerations for Adults and Seniors

Sleep needs and patterns continue to evolve throughout adulthood and into the senior years. Understanding these changes can help address sleep-related issues and promote better health and quality of life.

Sleep Considerations for Adults

Sleep Duration: Adults typically need 7-9 hours of sleep per night. However, individual needs can vary.

Common Sleep Disorders: Adults may experience sleep disorders such as insomnia, sleep apnea, and restless legs syndrome, which can affect sleep quality.

Impact of Lifestyle and Stress: Work-related stress, family responsibilities, and lifestyle choices can significantly impact sleep. Long working hours, shift work, and excessive use of caffeine and alcohol can disrupt sleep patterns.

Sleep Considerations for Seniors

Sleep Duration: Older adults typically need 7-8 hours of sleep per night, but sleep patterns can change with age.

Changes in Sleep Architecture: Seniors often experience changes in sleep architecture, with more frequent awakenings during the night and a decrease in deep sleep stages.

Common Sleep Disorders: Sleep disorders such as insomnia, sleep apnea, and periodic limb movement disorder are more prevalent in older adults. Additionally, conditions like chronic pain, arthritis, and medical issues can interfere with sleep.

Impact of Medications: Many seniors take medications that can affect sleep. It's important to review medications with a healthcare provider to identify potential side effects.

CHAPTER IX

Techniques for Better Sleep

Military Sleep Method

The "military method" is a technique used by the U.S. military to help soldiers fall asleep quickly, reportedly within 2 minutes or less, not necessarily 9 seconds. While achieving sleep in 9 seconds is likely an exaggeration, the method is designed to promote relaxation and prepare the body for sleep efficiently. Here's a breakdown of the military sleep method and some additional techniques for better sleep:

1. Relax Your Face:

Start by relaxing the muscles in your face, including your tongue, jaw, and the muscles around your eyes.
Let go of any tension and allow your face to go limp.

2. Drop Your Shoulders:

Let your shoulders drop as low as possible, releasing any tension.
Allow your arms to relax, one side at a time, starting from the upper arm down to your fingers.

3. Breathe and Relax Your Chest:

Take deep breaths and exhale slowly, relaxing your chest muscles as you do.

4. Relax Your Legs:

Start with your right thigh, letting it relax completely.
Move down to your calf, ankle, and foot.
Repeat the process with your left leg.

5. Clear Your Mind:

Imagine a relaxing scene, such as lying in a canoe on a calm lake with a clear blue sky above.

If your mind wanders, repeat the phrase "don't think" for about 10 seconds to help clear your thoughts.

By systematically relaxing your body and focusing on calm imagery or repetitive phrases, the military method aims to help you drift off to sleep more quickly.

Relaxation Techniques

Relaxation techniques are practices designed to reduce stress and promote a state of calmness. They can be particularly effective in improving sleep quality and helping individuals fall asleep faster. Here are some key relaxation techniques. The origins of relaxation techniques can be traced back to ancient civilizations. Around 1500 BCE, meditation practices began in India, documented in the Vedas, ancient Hindu scriptures. Yoga, which combines physical postures, breath control, and meditation, emerged from this tradition. These practices aimed to achieve spiritual enlightenment and physical well-being.

The Birth of Meditation in the East

Buddhism and Zen

In the 6th century BCE, Siddhartha Gautama, known as the Buddha, developed meditation techniques to attain enlightenment. His teachings spread throughout Asia, influencing Zen Buddhism in Japan. Zen meditation, or Zazen, focuses on mindful breathing and observation of thoughts, leading to mental clarity and relaxation.

Western Influence

The Relaxation Response

In the 20th century, Western medicine began to explore relaxation scientifically. Dr. Edmund Jacobson, an American physician, introduced Progressive Muscle Relaxation (PMR) in the 1920s. He believed that reducing muscle tension could alleviate anxiety. His method involved tensing and then relaxing different muscle groups, teaching the body to recognize and release stress.

Dr. Herbert Benson

In the 1970s, Dr. Herbert Benson, a cardiologist at Harvard Medical School, researched the effects of meditation on stress. He discovered what he called the "Relaxation Response," a state of deep rest that changes the physical and emotional responses to stress. His work popularized meditation and breathing techniques in the West as methods to combat stress and improve overall health.

Modern Techniques and Integration

Mindfulness-Based Stress Reduction (MBSR)

In the late 1970s, Jon Kabat-Zinn, a professor of medicine at the University of Massachusetts Medical School, developed Mindfulness-Based Stress Reduction (MBSR). MBSR integrates mindfulness meditation with yoga and body awareness, aiming to help individuals manage stress, pain, and illness. Kabat-Zinn's work has been widely influential, bringing mindfulness into mainstream medical and psychological practice.

The Role of Technology

Today, relaxation techniques have further evolved with the help of technology. Apps like Headspace and Calm provide guided meditations, breathing exercises, and sleep stories to millions of users worldwide. Virtual reality (VR) relaxation programs offer immersive experiences designed to reduce stress and promote relaxation.

CHAPTER X

Sleep and Mental Health

*"*Sleep is the golden chain that ties health and our bodies together."*"*

In the iconic film "American Psycho," Patrick Bateman, portrayed by Christian Bale, emerges as a haunting figure of 1980s excess and ambition. As a wealthy investment banker living in Manhattan, Bateman exudes success and charm. However, beneath his polished exterior lies a profound struggle with insomnia and deteriorating mental health. His sleeplessness becomes a harrowing symptom of a mind unraveling, fueling hallucinations, delusions, and a descent into violence. Patrick Bateman's portrayal vividly illustrates the profound interplay between sleep and mental health, showcasing how untreated issues can lead to a disturbing unraveling of sanity and stability.

Sleep and Mental Health: Understanding the Bidirectional Relationship

Sleep and mental health have a complex and bidirectional relationship, where each influences the other in significant ways. Understanding this relationship is crucial for maintaining overall well-being and effectively managing mental health disorders.

The Bidirectional Relationship

Impact of Mental Health on Sleep:

- Insomnia: Mental health disorders such as anxiety, depression, and PTSD often lead to insomnia, characterized by difficulty falling asleep or staying asleep.
- Sleep Disturbances: Conditions like bipolar disorder and schizophrenia can disrupt sleep patterns, causing irregular sleep-wake cycles and fragmented sleep.

Impact of Sleep on Mental Health:

- Mood Regulation: Adequate sleep plays a vital role in regulating mood and emotional responses. Sleep deprivation can lead to irritability, mood swings, and heightened emotional reactivity.
- Cognitive Function: Sleep is essential for cognitive functions such as attention, concentration, and decision-making. Chronic sleep deprivation can impair cognitive abilities and contribute to mental health challenges.

Sleep's Role in Stress Management

- Stress Response: Sleep helps regulate the body's stress response system. Adequate sleep enhances resilience to stressors and promotes emotional stability.
- Cortisol Regulation: During sleep, the body regulates cortisol levels, a hormone associated with stress. Chronic sleep deprivation disrupts this regulation, leading to elevated cortisol levels and increased stress.
- Psychological Resilience: Quality sleep enhances psychological resilience, making individuals better equipped to cope with stressors and adversity.

Sleep and Mental Health Disorders

Depression and Anxiety:

- Insomnia: Insomnia is a common symptom of depression and anxiety disorders. Sleep disturbances can exacerbate symptoms of these disorders, creating a cycle of sleep deprivation and worsening mental health. Managing insomnia is crucial as it can significantly impact an individual's overall well-being and daily functioning.
- Treatment Implications: Addressing sleep disturbances is essential in the treatment of depression and anxiety. Improving sleep quality can enhance treatment outcomes and reduce symptom severity. Therapies that focus on sleep hygiene and cognitive-behavioral techniques can be

particularly effective in breaking the cycle of poor sleep and mental health issues.

Bipolar Disorder:

- Sleep Patterns: Individuals with bipolar disorder often experience disruptions in sleep patterns, including insomnia during manic episodes and hypersomnia during depressive episodes.
- Stabilizing Mood: Establishing a regular sleep schedule and promoting healthy sleep habits can help stabilize mood and reduce the frequency of mood episodes.

PTSD (Post-Traumatic Stress Disorder):

- Nightmares and Flashbacks: Sleep disturbances, such as nightmares and flashbacks, are common in individuals with PTSD. These symptoms can interfere with sleep quality and contribute to daytime distress.
- Treatment Approaches: Cognitive Behavioral Therapy for Insomnia (CBT-I) and trauma-focused therapies are effective in addressing sleep disturbances and PTSD symptoms concurrently.

The relationship between sleep and mental health is intricate and multifaceted. Adequate sleep is essential for maintaining emotional well-being, cognitive function, and stress resilience. Conversely, mental health disorders often manifest through disturbances in sleep patterns, which can exacerbate symptoms and impair daily functioning.

Addressing sleep disturbances is a crucial aspect of managing and improving mental health outcomes. Incorporating strategies for better sleep hygiene, relaxation techniques, and seeking appropriate treatment for mental health disorders can significantly enhance overall well-being and quality of life. Recognizing and addressing the bidirectional relationship between sleep and mental health is essential for promoting optimal health and resilience across the lifespan.

CHAPTER XI

Sleep and Physical Health

LeBron James, one of the greatest basketball players of all time. LeBron is renowned not only for his exceptional talent on the court but also for his dedication to maintaining peak physical condition, which includes prioritizing sleep as a crucial component of his regimen. In his early career, LeBron James struggled with managing his sleep schedule due to the demands of training, games, and media obligations. Like many athletes, he initially underestimated the impact of sleep on his performance and recovery. As LeBron matured in his career, he began working closely with sports scientists and trainers who emphasized the importance of sleep for optimal performance. Recognizing the benefits, LeBron made significant lifestyle adjustments to ensure he received adequate rest each night.

Integrating Sleep into Routine

LeBron James implemented several strategies to prioritize sleep:

- **Consistent Sleep Schedule:** He established a consistent bedtime and wake-up time, even during the NBA season's demanding schedule.
- **Sleep Environment:** LeBron created an optimal sleep environment, including using blackout curtains, controlling room temperature, and minimizing noise and light disruptions.
- **Recovery Focus:** LeBron viewed sleep as critical for recovery. After intense games or workouts, he prioritized restorative sleep to facilitate muscle repair and mental rejuvenation.

Performance and Longevity Benefits

LeBron James credits his improved performance and longevity in the NBA to prioritizing sleep. By ensuring he gets 8-10 hours of quality sleep each night, LeBron enhances his reaction time, cognitive function, and overall physical endurance. His commitment to sleep has not only sustained his athletic excellence but also contributed to his longevity and ability to maintain peak performance well into his 30s and beyond. LeBron has often emphasized that adequate rest is as crucial as training and nutrition in his regimen. This focus on sleep allows him to recover more effectively from intense workouts and games, reducing the risk of injury. Consequently,

LeBron's dedication to sleep has become a cornerstone of his remarkable career and enduring success.

Sleep and Physical Health

Sleep plays a crucial role in physical health across various aspects, including its impact on chronic diseases, immune system support, and weight management.

Impact on Chronic Diseases

Consistent poor sleep is linked to a higher risk of chronic diseases such as diabetes, cardiovascular disease, and hypertension. Sleep deprivation or poor quality sleep can disrupt physiological processes like glucose metabolism, hormone regulation (including insulin), and blood pressure control. Over time, these disruptions contribute to the development or exacerbation of chronic conditions.

Immune System Support Through Sleep

Quality sleep is essential for a robust immune system. During sleep, the body produces and releases cytokines, a type of protein that helps the immune system respond effectively against infections and inflammation. Chronic sleep deprivation can reduce the production of these protective cytokines and impair immune function, increasing susceptibility to illnesses like the common cold or flu.

Weight Management and Sleep

Sleep and metabolism are closely intertwined. Sleep deprivation disrupts the balance of key hormones that regulate appetite, ghrelin (which stimulates appetite), and leptin (which signals fullness). This imbalance can lead to increased hunger and cravings for high-calorie foods, which in turn can contribute to weight gain. Moreover, inadequate sleep can affect the body's ability to process and store carbohydrates, leading to higher blood sugar levels and potentially increasing the risk of insulin resistance.

"Simone Biles is an American artistic gymnast known for her exceptional talent and multiple Olympic gold medals. Throughout her career, Biles has emphasized the importance of maintaining a balanced approach to training, nutrition, and rest."

Biles, like many elite athletes, faces the challenge of managing her weight while ensuring she gets enough sleep to support her rigorous training schedule. As a gymnast, maintaining strength, agility, and endurance is crucial, and adequate rest plays a vital role in her recovery and performance.

To address these challenges, Biles works closely with her coaches and a team of sports nutritionists and sleep specialists. They have developed a tailored nutrition plan that includes sufficient calories to fuel her intense training sessions while ensuring she maintains a healthy weight. The plan focuses on nutrient-dense foods that provide the energy and nutrients her body needs to perform at its best.

In terms of sleep, Biles prioritizes getting enough rest each night to support her recovery. She follows a consistent sleep schedule and practices good sleep hygiene, such as creating a relaxing bedtime routine and ensuring her sleep environment is conducive to rest. Biles understands that quality sleep is essential not only for physical recovery but also for mental focus and emotional well-being.

Simone Biles' dedication to balancing weight management with optimal sleep exemplifies how elite athletes can achieve success by prioritizing their overall health and well-being. Her approach underscores the importance of a holistic approach to training that considers the interconnectedness of nutrition, sleep, and athletic performance.

CHAPTER XII

Creating Healthy Sleep Habits

In our fast-paced world, where demands and distractions abound, cultivating healthy sleep habits is crucial for our overall well-being. Let's explore three essential strategies to help you achieve restorative and refreshing sleep.

Developing a Sleep Routine

Establishing a consistent sleep routine is foundational to promoting healthy sleep patterns. Here's how you can create an effective routine:

Set a Consistent Bedtime: Aim to go to bed and wake up at the same time every day, even on weekends, to regulate your body's internal clock.

Create a Relaxing Bedtime Ritual: Engage in calming activities before bed, such as reading, taking a warm bath, or practicing relaxation techniques like deep breathing or meditation.

Limit Stimulants and Screen Time: Avoid caffeine and heavy meals close to bedtime, and reduce exposure to screens (phones, tablets, computers) at least an hour before sleep, as the blue light can interfere with your body's production of melatonin, a hormone that regulates sleep.

Developing a consistent sleep routine helps signal to your body that it's time to wind down, making it easier to fall asleep and wake up feeling refreshed.

Sleep Journaling

Keeping a sleep journal can provide valuable insights into your sleep patterns and habits. Here's how to start:

Record Sleep Patterns: Track the time you go to bed, how long it takes you to fall asleep, and how many times you wake up during the night.

Note Sleep Quality: Rate your sleep quality on a scale from 1 to 10, noting any factors that may have affected it, such as stress, caffeine intake, or late-night activities.

Identify Patterns and Triggers: Over time, you may notice trends or triggers that affect your sleep, such as certain foods, activities, or stressors.

Use this information to make adjustments to your sleep routine.

Sleep journaling can empower you to make informed decisions about your sleep habits and identify areas where improvement is needed.

Seeking Professional Help When Needed

Sometimes, despite our best efforts, sleep issues persist or worsen. Seeking professional help from a healthcare provider or sleep specialist can be instrumental in identifying and addressing underlying sleep disorders or chronic insomnia. Here's when to consider professional help:

Persistent Sleep Problems: If you consistently have difficulty falling asleep, staying asleep, or waking up too early despite following healthy sleep practices.

Daytime Impairment: If poor sleep quality is affecting your daily functioning, mood, or overall health.

Unusual Symptoms: If you experience symptoms such as loud snoring, pauses in breathing during sleep, or excessive daytime sleepiness that may indicate sleep apnea or other sleep disorders.

A healthcare provider can conduct a thorough evaluation, recommend appropriate treatments or therapies, and provide personalized guidance to help you achieve better sleep and overall health.

By integrating these strategies into your lifestyle, you can create and maintain healthy sleep habits that promote restful nights and energized days. Remember, sleep is essential for physical, mental, and emotional well-being, and investing in good sleep hygiene is an investment in your overall quality of life.

CHAPTER XIII

Sleep Patterns of Drowsy Creatures

Welcome to the whimsical world of sleep—where creatures great and small find ingenious ways to rest and recharge. From the deep slumber of bears in winter's embrace to the perpetual motion of Arctic terns crossing oceans, each species has its own tale to tell about how it sleeps and survives. Join us as we explore the fascinating sleep patterns of some of nature's most drowsy denizens!

Bears:

Hibernation: Bears are well-known for their ability to hibernate through the winter months. During hibernation, their metabolic rate slows dramatically, and they enter a state of torpor where they can go without eating, drinking, urinating, or defecating for months.

Types of Bears: Different species exhibit varying degrees of hibernation. For example, black bears in milder climates may not hibernate as deeply as polar bears in the Arctic.

Bats:

Nocturnal Lifestyle: Bats are nocturnal creatures, meaning they are most active during the night. They spend daylight hours roosting in caves, trees, or buildings.

Sleeping Upside Down: Bats have a unique adaptation for sleep—they hang upside down! This posture allows them to take off quickly and efficiently if they sense danger.

Dolphins:

Unihemispheric Slow-wave Sleep (USWS): Dolphins exhibit a fascinating sleep behavior called unihemispheric slow-wave sleep. This means they sleep with one hemisphere of their brain at a time, while the other remains awake and alert.

Constant Vigilance: By maintaining some level of consciousness at all times, dolphins can continue swimming, avoid predators, and ensure they surface to breathe regularly.

Giraffes:

Short, Light Sleep: Giraffes sleep for short periods of time throughout the day and night, totaling about 4.6 hours on average. They often sleep standing up or lying down, with their long necks and powerful legs allowing them to quickly wake and flee from danger.

Vigilance: Even while sleeping, giraffes are vigilant due to their vulnerability to predators like lions.

Elephants:

Minimal Sleep: Elephants have relatively short sleep cycles compared to their size, sleeping for about 4 hours a day, usually at night.

Standing or Lying Down: Similar to giraffes, elephants can sleep standing up or lying down. Their large size and herd structure provide protection while they rest.

Hedgehogs:

Hibernation: Hedgehogs are known to hibernate during the winter months in colder regions. Their body temperature drops significantly, and they enter a state of torpor to conserve energy until temperatures rise.

Sloths:

Slow Metabolism: Sloths are famous for their slow movements and equally slow metabolism. They spend up to 20 hours a day sleeping or resting, often hanging upside down from trees, which conserves energy and minimizes their exposure to predators.

Energy Conservation: Their slow pace and low-energy lifestyle help them survive on a diet of leaves, which are low in nutrients. This adaptation allows sloths to conserve energy and thrive in their arboreal habitats, despite their low-calorie diet.

Whales:

Unihemispheric Sleep: Like dolphins, some whale species exhibit unihemispheric slow-wave sleep. This adaptation allows them to continue swimming, surfacing for air, and maintaining awareness of their surroundings even while sleeping.

Birds (e.g., Ducks):

Unihemispheric Sleep: Many bird species, such as ducks, can sleep with one hemisphere of their brain at a time. This allows them to stay alert for predators and environmental changes, especially important for species that live in open habitats.

Cats:

Polyphasic Sleep: Domestic cats and many wild feline species are polyphasic sleepers, meaning they sleep multiple times throughout the day and night. They can quickly enter a state of alertness when needed, making them effective predators.

Sharks:

Continuous Movement: Some shark species, like the great white shark, need to swim continuously to pass water over their gills for oxygen. They exhibit periods of rest where they slow down and become less responsive, but they do not enter a true sleep state as mammals do.

Owls:

Nocturnal Hunters: Owls are nocturnal birds of prey known for their exceptional night vision and silent flight. They sleep during the day in hidden, quiet locations, relying on their camouflage for protection.

Horses:

Light Sleepers: Horses are herbivorous mammals that sleep for short periods of time throughout the day and night. They can doze standing up or lying down, often in groups for safety.

Cows:

Rumination: Cows are ruminant animals that spend a lot of time eating and ruminating (chewing cud). They have a unique sleep pattern where they sleep for short periods, often standing up, and ruminate during rest.

Koalas:

Nocturnal with Long Naps: Koalas are arboreal marsupials native to Australia. They sleep for up to 18-22 hours a day, primarily to conserve energy from their low-nutrient diet of eucalyptus leaves.

Snakes:

Variability: Snakes have diverse sleep patterns depending on their species and habitat. Some are nocturnal, while others are diurnal (active during the day). Snakes can also enter a state of torpor to conserve energy during periods of cold weather or food scarcity.

Gorillas:

Nest Builders: Gorillas are large primates that construct nests for sleeping at night. They typically sleep in nests made from leaves and branches, usually in trees or on the ground depending on the species.

Bees:

Cluster Sleeping: Honeybees and other social bee species exhibit cluster sleeping, where they gather together in groups within their hive. This behavior helps them maintain warmth and protect the queen bee and brood.

Squirrels:

Light Sleepers: Squirrels are diurnal rodents known for their quick movements and agile behavior. They sleep in short bursts throughout the day and night, often in nests or dens they build in trees or underground.

Arctic Terns:

Continuous Migration: Arctic terns are seabirds known for their incredible migratory journeys. During migration, they can fly non-stop for thousands of miles, often sleeping in short periods while gliding over the ocean.

As we explore the sleep patterns of these fascinating creatures, we're reminded that sleep reflects the remarkable diversity and adaptability of life on Earth. Whether bats hanging upside down or Arctic terns migrating endlessly, each species has evolved unique strategies for survival. So, next time you settle in for sleep, consider the myriad ways our fellow inhabitants find rest, as diverse and intriguing as the creatures themselves.